W9-CFR-802

Introduction to Teachers

We all know the importance of teaching students to write clear, well-structured essays. After all, the essay is the basis of most academic writing. But we also know that teaching essay writing is not easy. Ask students to write a story or a poem, and more often than not they will enjoy the task. Unfortunately, essays are often synonymous with boredom and labor. They don't have to be.

The purpose of this book is twofold: (1) to teach students step-by-step how to write a five-paragraph essay and (2) to demonstrate the creativity and fun involved in essay writing. We must be able to show students that although expository writing is hard work, the process can be an enjoyable and creative one. Students must learn that expository essays can be engaging; they can be funny, dramatic, and personal.

How to Write an Essay is process oriented. Students begin by learning to gather and shape ideas and then to move into structuring their papers. This is followed by some instruction on writing itself, including paragraphing and transitions, along with introductions and conclusions. From there, students draft their pieces and then revise them.

The reading component of *How to Write an Essay* is important. Students are asked to peer edit one another's work, read and respond to two model essays, and keep a reading journal. These steps need some explanation:

- *Peer Editing:* Students will read and respond to one another's work during the writing process and also after they complete their papers. This peer response is very important, for it allows students to learn from one another and to see different writing styles and possibilities. While it will take some encouragement and practice to get students to respond with constructive criticism, it is a worthwhile struggle. The teacher should not be the only person evaluating and appreciating a student's work. By interacting with his or her peers, the student will find more meaning in the writing process. Editing that is restricted to the teacher-to-student response is isolating for both.

- *Model Essays:* These appear at the back of the book (pages 39–42), along with response questions. When to introduce these essays is left to your discretion. They are high quality five-paragraph essays that show how rich the form can be. This richness is within the reach of most middle school students.

- *Reading Journal:* After reading pages 6 and 7, you will need to decide whether or not keeping a reading journal is appropriate for your class. A decision to keep a journal represents an ongoing commitment to supplement this book with published essays and to respond to those essays. The benefits of such a journal are obvious, but it does require work on your part and on the students' part. You will need to take trips to the library, provide in-class resources, and allow students to share their readings.

Introduction to Teachers *(cont.)*

Rubrics, which appear at the end of the section on outlining (pages 17–20), are another important feature of this book. Rubrics allow for a more holistic evaluation of the essay writing process and the finished product. By focusing on specific elements, the rubric encourages students to focus on improvement. Students use the rubric models to evaluate one another's work along the way. Letter grading is left to your discretion. *However, it is essential that you provide specific feedback to your students as they develop their papers.* A letter grade for the final product may be appropriate, but if it is the sole response, it doesn't give the students much to work with. Rubrics provide a healthy alternative.

Teaching Suggestions

- Use an overhead projector to display writing and to generate discussion. This allows the class an opportunity to read and respond together. Consider featuring a model essay and slowly reading and responding to its features.

- Bring professional writers into your classroom. This might be difficult to do, but it's very worthwhile. When students meet people who write for a living, when they see firsthand that writing matters in the "real world," the process has more meaning. Consider contacting your local newspaper. Is there an editor or reporter willing to visit your classroom?

- Create an "Essays" bulletin board that features student and published work. This doesn't have to be limited to finished products. If someone comes up with a particularly engaging introduction, for example, why not feature it on the board? You can also highlight each part of the essay writing process: brainstorming, outlining, and so forth.

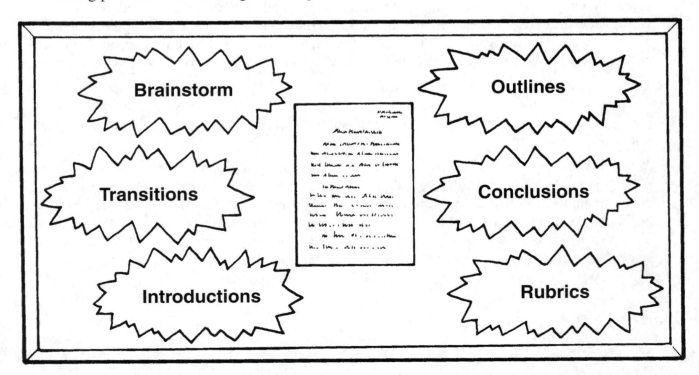

Introduction

In the next few weeks, you will be learning how to write a five-paragraph expository essay. *Expository* means the essay should explain or give information. So, you can write an expository essay about trains or dinosaurs or dreams—anything that can be explained or explored is fine.

As you continue in your schooling, you will find that the essay—whether it be a persuasive essay, an interpretive essay, or a research paper—is the basis of most writing assignments. Furthermore, writing essays isn't limited to English class; you'll write them for history, anthropology, and even science. So, you are taking a very valuable step here.

While you learn the skills involved, it's important that you find out that essay writing can be fun. As you will see, your essay can do a good job of providing information and still be creative.

What to Expect

This book explain to you how to write a five-paragraph essay, step by step. You will begin by finding and developing a topic. Then you will learn how to structure your ideas. Next, you will learn some writing tips, how to write a rough draft, and finally how to prepare a revised final draft. When you finish, you will be asked to present your essay. You will also join your classmates in producing a class anthology of essays!

How to Write an Essay is not a guide to grammar or punctuation. Instead, it focuses on what it takes to write a clear, well-structured, interesting essay. There are lots of opportunities to work with classmates. In fact, you will be responding directly to one another's material as you develop your essay.

Before You Begin

Before you start, it's important to discuss and write down how you feel about writing. This will give you a "fresh start." Take 15 minutes and write down how you feel about writing. Consider the following questions:

- Do you like to write? Why or why not?

- What kind of writing is your favorite?

- What is an essay? What comes to mind when you think of essay writing?

- How do you feel about your writing abilities?

- How can the class and the teacher best help you along?

When you have finished writing, discuss your responses in a peer group or with your whole class. This will give you a "fresh start" to begin writing your essay. Good luck!

Reading and the Reading Journal

Reading is one of the best ways to learn about writing. By reading stories, we learn how plots are shaped and characters developed. Reading poetry introduces us to the various forms and rhythms of verse. Likewise, by reading essays, we learn about the structures and ideas involved. We see the array of topics essay writing covers, from "Foods on the Oregon Trail" to "How to Interpret Your Dreams in Three Easy Steps." We also see how the writing can be friendly, dramatic, funny, and creative—not just straightforward.

The more published essays you read, the more you will learn about and, hopefully, the more you will appreciate the form. Of course, most of the essays you find won't be in five-paragraph form, but they will follow the same principles: They will be clearly written and well organized. To help you with this, we are providing two model essays to study, along with response questions to get you thinking about them. Your teacher will decide when to introduce these essays.

So, with the help of your teacher and librarian, start finding and reading published essays. *You should be reading at least two essays per week as you learn to write your own.* The list of young adult magazines that follows is a good resource, but you shouldn't limit yourself to these. There are lots of magazines and newspapers that feature essays that might interest you. Are there magazines devoted to your favorite hobby? Did you know there are magazines devoted solely to snowboarding? And magazines all about cooking?

Bring your essays into class and share them with other students. If there's one in particular that interests you, get it copied for your classmates or present it to them. Discussing essays is a real plus in learning about the form and improving your reading skills.

The Reading Journal

To complement your essay reading, you should keep a reading journal which will include responses to essays and articles you read. Naturally, you will summarize and respond to the essay: What was it about? Did you enjoy it? But you will also go further.

In the following weeks, you will learn about the steps involved in writing an essay. Pay attention to these elements in the essays you read. For example, if you're practicing using effective transitions (pages 24 and 25), look closely at the way the essayist uses transitions. When you study "intended audience" (pages 21 and 22), consider the author's audience. *Write your impressions in your reading journal.* By reflecting on the specifics of an essay, you'll learn better and pick up some tips.

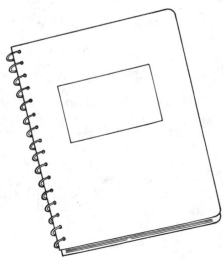

Feel free to decorate your reading journal with photos, illustrations, and so forth. If you are diligent about this project, it will pay off! Your reading skills will improve, as will your essay writing.

Reading and the Reading Journal *(cont.)*

Reading Resources

The following list of top publications can be a beginning for anyone looking for some good essays to read. You can be sure that they will be interesting, filled with specific details, and provide you with many good examples to model your writing on.

Once again, remember that this list represents only a starting point. Ask your librarian, teacher, and parents for help in finding other sources. Also, don't limit yourself to magazines for kids or young adults. You might find some wonderful, highly readable essays in magazines for adults.

* *Creative with Words Publications.* Box 223225, Carmel, CA 93922-3226

* *Cricket.* 315 5th Street, Box 3000, Peru, IL 61354

* *Merlyn's Pen, The National Magazine of Student Writing.* Box 1058, East Greenwich, RI 02818

* *New Moon.* P.O. Box 3587, Duluth, MN 55803

* *Sports Illustrated for Kids.* Time-Life Bldg., Rockefeller Center, New York, NY 10020

* *Stone Soup: The Magazine for Young Writers and Artists.* P.O. Box 83, Santa Cruz, CA 95063

* *Time for Kids—World Report.* Time-Life Bldg., Rockefeller Center, New York, NY 10020

* *Teen People.* Time-Life Bldg., Rockefeller Center, New York, NY 10020

* *National Geographic World.* P.O. Box 98002, Washington, D.C. 20090-8002

Finding a Topic

The first step in writing an essay is deciding on your topic. For some students that is an easy step, while others struggle. Have you ever found yourself saying, "I don't know what to write about"? Or you decide on one topic, and then the next day you change your mind? Fortunately, there are some steps that might make finding a topic a smooth and painless experience.

Before we practice these, however, we have to ask ourselves what kinds of topics are appropriate for an expository essay. Remember that an expository essay explains or gives information about a topic. You could simply write about your favorite sport or about three kinds of spiders that live in your neighborhood.

Remember that this information can highlight something about the topic. In other words, you can have an *angle* on your topic. For example, if you write an essay about the nature of tornadoes, you can also be doing so as a warning to those of us who live in tornado country. Therefore, the information serves a purpose. Later, we will go into this more deeply.

Does this mean you can write about anything? Yes and no. There are three points to consider:

- Since you will be writing only five paragraphs, you don't want your topic to be too general. For example, "Earth" is probably too wide a topic. Can you narrow it? How about "Continents." That might work, but how about "South America?" Is there a country in South America that you have always wondered about? What about Brazil? "Yes," you think to yourself, "I have a friend from Brazil who lives on a farm. He visits every summer." A five-paragraph essay about Brazil would be terrific!

- That brings up our second point: Choose a topic that interests you and leaves some room for discovery. A topic that requires at least a little research (see pages 15 and 16) will help keep your momentum flowing.

- You also don't want to choose a topic that's too narrow. If you do, you'll find it hard to develop your topic. In such a case there may not be enough available information, the information may be too detailed and complex, or else it may be too simple and self-evident. For example, it might be difficult to write an essay on the sleeping positions of hibernating bears! "Hibernation" is more suitable, and there is plenty of information to find on the topic.

Finding a Topic: The Focus Ladder

One way to help you choose a topic is to create a focus ladder. This exercise helps you find details, too. We will explore this further on the following pages. Let's study the focus ladder in the following example to see how this works.

General:	food
Specific:	food for humans
More Specific:	health food for humans
Topic:	Health Food for Kids

The process is simple: You begin with a general topic and then get more specific until you find a topic that works. "Health Food for Kids" is a wonderful choice for a five-paragraph essay. Since you eat healthful food, you want to show others that they can also by providing examples of tasty food that's also good for you. You can discuss foods for breakfast, lunch, or dinner, or you can discuss the different food groups and healthy options in each of them. In some cases, your focus ladder will be more than four lines.

Here are three topics to begin practicing focus ladders. These might lead to the topic you use for your essay. Below the three practice topics are spaces for you to supply two more of your own topics. Begin with a general topic that interests you and go from there!

Note: You should complete these exercises even if you have a topic already.

General	Outer Space	Animals	Entertainment
Specific			
More Specific			
Topic			

Your Own Topics

General		
Specific		
More Specific		
Topic		

Brainstorming

For many people, starting is the most challenging part of writing an essay. Have you ever sat in front of a blank piece of paper (or blank computer screen) and felt like filling it with words would be an impossible task? Have you ever felt as if you have nothing to write about? If so, you're not alone. Here are some strategies that will help.

One of the best ways to think of ideas is to use *brainstorming*. When you play basketball or go jogging, you prepare by shooting the ball or stretching. Brainstorming serves this same purpose. Instead of feeling the pressure to start writing right away, you can relax and write down all the associations that come to mind about your topic.

Here are the steps to follow when brainstorming:

* Get a large piece of construction paper. Make sure you have plenty of room to write.

* In the center of the paper, write your topic, and then circle it.

* Spend at least 20–30 minutes writing down *everything* that comes to mind. Don't edit! Don't worry about writing something "wrong." You may scribble something that you don't think you will use, only to find that it leads you to a wonderful detail you had not thought of. Like warming up for sports, your ideas will start to free themselves up, and you will start gathering momentum.

* No idea is wrong. Even if you feel silly writing an idea, even if you are sure it won't fit into your essay, write it down!

Study the sample brainstorm about health foods for kids on the following page. Notice the variety of ideas that are generated. Some aren't directly related to the topic, but they might be useful. The ideas are plentiful, so now the writer has some materials to use. As you will see, it's the *details* that bring your essay to life, so spend lots of time on this assignment.

Brainstorming with a Partner

Brainstorming with a partner is fun and useful. It provides twice the "firepower." There are a couple of ways to do this: (1) Write together. Make room for both people to write simultaneously, sharing ideas, or (2) each of you writes a brainstorm on the *same topic* separately. When you're done, come together and see what you have included that the other person hasn't. Then fuse the topics together.

Brainstorming as a Class

The teacher takes control here. Using the overhead projector or writing on a chalkboard, your teacher writes ideas that the class offers.

Brainstorming (cont.)

Sample Brainstorm

Kids need to learn to eat healthful foods.

Everyone thinks healthy food tastes bad.

Oatmeal

It's not all "health food."

What about desserts?

Granola

Those Rice Dream things are pretty good.

Avoid fast food places.

Fruit rules!

Sesame sticks are pretty good.

What is cholesterol, anyway?

High cholesterol?

Peanut butter is healthy.

My Uncle Charlie eats everything in sight and he seems pretty healthy, but I bet it'll catch up with him.

I can't stand persimmons.

Kids think that bad eating habits won't affect them.

Potato chips without salt and all the oily junk are okay.

Salad

But not too much salad dressing.

It tastes great, though.

Try to eat organic stuff.

Organic stuff is more expensive.

Pasta

Preservatives are bad for you.

Garden burgers instead of too many hamburgers.

How do preservatives work?

Vitamins (Do these count as food?)

Cola is pretty bad for you.

Exercise is important, too.

I wonder if those natural sodas are really "natural."

I heard running isn't too good for your knees, though.

There was this news show about kids being allergic to peanut butter.

It's hard to be perfect.

Brainstorming *(cont.)*

Brainstorming A to Z

Another helpful brainstorming strategy is to cover your topic from A to Z. The guidelines are simple: For each letter of the alphabet, write down an idea that relates to your topic and begins with that letter.

Some of the letters might be hard to match with ideas. That's why this is a perfect opportunity to use reference books such as the encyclopedia and the dictionary. If you still cannot find an idea for the letter X, that's okay—just do your best.

Here is a sample A-to-Z list under another topic—Abraham Lincoln.

A. Appomattox Court House
B. Booth, John Wilkes
C. Civil War
D. Douglas, Stephen A.
E. Emancipation Proclamation
F. Ford's Theater
G. Gettysburg Address
H. Honest Abe
I. Illinois
J. Johnson, Andrew
K. Kansas-Nebraska Act
L. Lawyer
M. Missouri Compromise
N. Nancy Lincoln
O. *Our American Cousin*
P. President
Q. Quotable
R. Republican
S. Slavery
T. Todd, Mary
U. Union
V. Virginia
W. Whig
X. XVIth president
Y. Yankees
Z. Zealous

Any area of the A-to-Z list (or several areas combined) can now be the focus for writing on the topic. The discussion and illustration of webbing on pages 13 and 14 will help you to organize the details from your brainstorming.

Webbing and Freewriting

Now that you have a flood of ideas before you, you're ready for the next steps: *webbing* and *freewriting*. Webbing invites you to make connections between the details and ideas in your brainstorm, while freewriting gets your ideas flowing and your creative spark moving. You can begin your web in one of two ways: (1) You can use a fresh piece of paper and add details from your brainstorm, or (2) you can write directly on your brainstorm. Study the web on the following page. Notice the connections between ideas. These are called *idea clusters*. As you draw your web, you are looking for ideas and details that are related. Of course, lots of material will overlap, so don't be surprised if some details fall into more than one idea cluster. When you complete the web, you will discover that *it suggests structure for your paper*. It will show you which details are essential to your essay and which ones can be left out. In this case we broke the details into clusters representing breakfast, lunch, and dinner.

Freewriting is useful at any time but especially when just beginning your writing. There is only one rule: Using what you know about your topic, take out a piece of paper and WRITE! Forget about spelling and punctuation. Just keep going! Like brainstorming, this process frees up your ideas and keeps the "I-don't-like-that-idea" voice quiet. Write for 15 minutes minimum. If you don't know what to write, write "I don't know what to write," until you get on a new train of thought. When you are done, you should have at least a page written about your topic, and you will probably find useful material in there.

You can use the freewriting method any time in the essay-writing process, especially if you're feeling stuck or when you are just sitting down to write. Here's an example from a freewriting session.

> Oh well here goes. I want to write about photography. I think the first camera was invented in the 1800s or something like that, and I know people had to stay still for a long time while the picture was taken. I remember seeing pictures of Civil War soldiers and when they moved. Things sure have changed now that they have digital cameras. Old time pictures were called daguerrotypes or something like that. What a weird word. I wonder what they would think knowing that now we can take a picture and have the camera, like one of those polaroids, just spit out the picture. I like nature photography best, but it always makes me want to be at the place I see, like a waterfall or something like that.

Webbing and Freewriting *(cont.)*

Web Page

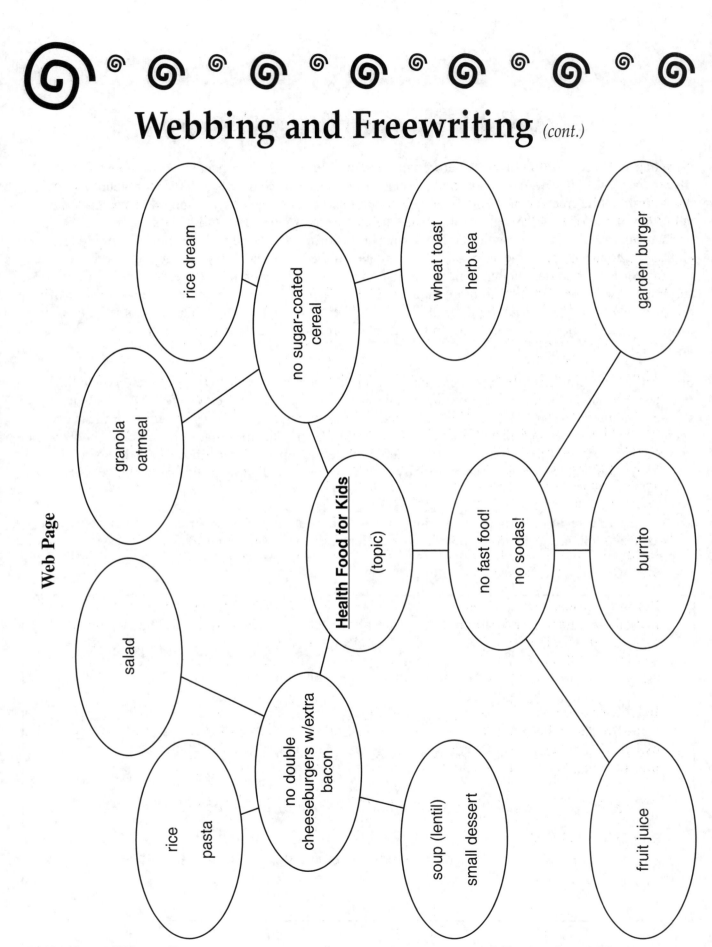

Finding Information

Even if you already know a great deal about your topic, it is always useful to find out more. There is bound to be a new fact that you haven't considered. In our "Health Food for Kids" paper, for example, the writer might go to a food company's Web site to discover a new tasty alternative to chocolate just out on the market. That kind of detail would enrich the essay and impress the reader.

Locating Your Resources

Naturally, if you need more information, taking some time to research is important. This might mean a trip to the library. Here are some resources to consider using in your search for facts and ideas.

- Dictionaries: You will be surprised how useful a good dictionary can be and how many different kinds of dictionaries there are! (There are even Websites that you can use. Mirriam-Webster is one source at http://word@M-W.com.) Begin by looking up your topic or a related word and studying its definitions. Then look more deeply into its etymology. The *etymology* of a word explains its origin, how it came to be. If you were writing a paper on the Gold Rush, for example, with some research you might discover that the cry of *Eureka*! has its origins in a Greek story involving the philosopher Archimedes and the crown of King Heiro. (Look it up—it's a great story!) In this case, you will have to search for a special dictionary that focuses on word origins. Ask your librarian for help searching the reference section.

- Encyclopedias: These are also terrific sources. Again, it is worth a trip to the library just to see the different kinds of encyclopedias. Of course, you have the general ones, but there are also encyclopedias devoted solely to plant life or to music.

- Books: Consider finding older books about your topic. You might find some wonderful material to compare and contrast with newer facts. For example, if you were composing an essay about Prohibition, a book about the subject written in the 1920s would be fascinating, wouldn't it? There could be some dramatic or even funny quotes that you could use in your essay.

- Interviews: Do you know an expert on your topic? If you are writing about helmet laws, could you call a lawyer or law enforcement official and ask him or her some questions? An expert will probably have a fresh perspective on your topic or be able to add some useful information. Also, you could quote the person, adding more variety to your essay.

Note: If you interview someone, don't overuse the information. For example, if two-thirds of your essay is quotes from an expert on helmet laws, you have gone too far. Use the information sparingly.

Finding Information *(cont.)*

Locating Your Resources *(cont.)*

- Internet: The Internet has become an excellent tool for research. There are thousands of Web sites about thousands of topics. One warning: Be sure that your information is reliable. Information from a chat room, for instance, may not be suitable. Likewise, there are countless personal and business Web sites with information that might not be well-researched. Check with your teacher about suitability.

Documenting Your Information

When doing research for your essay, it is essential that you write down your sources. Then when you present a statistic, a fact, or a quote, you can prove where you got the information. So, make sure that you have a list of your sources. If it is a dictionary or book, write down the title, the author and/or editors, the copyright date, and the page(s) you got the information from. If it is a Web site, write down the whole address. And if you interview someone, write down the date of the interview and the person's name.

Your teacher will let you know the best place to list your sources. Usually they appear on a separate piece of paper called a *bibliography*. A bibliography is helpful because it shows where you got your information; if the person reading your essay wants to explore the topic further, he or she knows where to begin.

Research Warm Up: "Three New Facts" Collage

Here is a group project that is lots of fun. You will need a little research, a piece of construction paper, some colored pens, scissors, glue or tape, and old magazines.

(1) Whether you will use this new information for your essay or not, you need to find at least three facts about your topic that you did not know before you began your research. Even if you fancy yourself an expert, there will be new information out there!

(2) After everyone has three facts, you need to make a *visual representation* of them. If you find new statistics on helmet injuries among ten to thirteen-year-olds, for example, you could draw a graph illustrating you findings. If you discover that Mount Whitney is the tallest mountain in the Continental United States, you could cut out a photo of a mountain from a magazine.

(3) Now create a "Three New Facts" collage that includes your visual representation *and* a written statement of your fact. Below the magazine photo of a mountain for example, you could write, "Mount Whitney is the highest mountain in the Continental United States."

(4) When you are done, decorate your classroom with the collages.

Outlining

Writing an essay is a lot like building a house. Right now you have all your ideas but no order to them. This is like having your tools and building supplies but no blueprint for your house. In both cases, if you begin without a plan, you are liable to create something that is disordered. Your house will have a triangular living room, and your paper will leap from one topic to another without any sense of direction.

This is when an *outline* comes in handy. The purpose of an outline is to order your ideas so that your paper has a meaningful and logical structure. There are many choices to make when outlining, just as there are many different ways to outline the same topic. We will focus on a very basic form of the outline. As you will see, it's a worthwhile task, for once you have your ideas in order, you can focus on the writing of the essay without worrying about the structure. It's just like the builder who looks at his or her blueprints and then begins to build.

Look at the sample outline on the following page. This is the model you will be using for your five-paragraph essay. Let's take one element at a time.

- **Topic:** Write down your topic in one concise statement or question. Here, it appears as "Health Food for Kids." If it helps, write it as a question: "What Are Some Health Foods for Kids?"

- **Introduction:** The introduction functions as the first paragraph of your essay. Later, you will learn more about writing introductions and conclusions. In the outline, there is no need to develop either the introduction or the conclusion. They are meant as markers for the structure. However, you may want to add your "hooks" to your outline (see pages 26–28).

- **Main Idea:** As you can see, there are three main ideas on the outline. These represent the body of the essay, which means everything except the introduction and conclusion. The main ideas are the building blocks or centerpieces of your paper. You will need to study your mind map to divide the paper into three logical parts. Each main idea must support your topic. The main ideas should be more specific than the topic but general enough to merit development. In this case, we have divided the paper into the three meals of the day.

- **Details:** For each of the main ideas, you add three details. Notice how the details support and develop the main idea. This is where your brainstorming and research come in handy.

- **Conclusion:** Like the introduction in the outline, the conclusion is meant as a marker. See pages 26–28 for tips on how to write an effective conclusion.

Outlining *(cont.)*

Sample Outline

Topic: Health Food for Kids

Introduction: Not all foods that kids eat . . .

Main Idea: Breakfast

- Detail: granola

- Detail: "Rice Dream" instead of milk

- Detail: oatmeal

Main Idea: Lunch

- Detail: garden burgers

- Detail: burrito

- Detail: fruit

Main Idea: Dinner

- Detail: salad

- Detail: lentil soup

- Detail: pasta

Conclusion: There are several alternatives . . .

Outlining *(cont.)*

My Outline

Topic: _____

Introduction:

Main Idea: _____

- Detail: _____

- Detail: _____

- Detail: _____

Main Idea: _____

- Detail: _____

- Detail: _____

- Detail: _____

Main Idea: _____

- Detail: _____

- Detail: _____

- Detail: _____

Conclusion:

Outlining (cont.)

Outlining Rubric

The purpose of an outlining rubric is to help you judge whether your outline or essay is good or whether it needs more work before you submit it. In other words, the rubric helps you score your outline and/or essay. This is helpful for the writer of the essay and also for any peer editors who are reading their work. Teachers use rubrics to help score writing of many kinds, but especially for essays.

Simply look at the descriptive statements in each section of the rubric and compare them to your essay. If all the descriptive statements in the Score 3 category match your essay, for example, that is the score your essay should receive. Using a rubric like this helps you to be specific and uniform in your judgment. Everybody's essays can then be judged by the same fair standards.

Score 3: High Pass
* Essay topic is focused—not too general or too narrow.
* There are three clear and defined main ideas.
* All three main ideas support the topic.
* Each paragraph contains three interesting details.
* All details are clearly related to the main idea.
* All details are succinct, interesting. No overlap.
* Outline is presented neatly with no writing errors.

Score 2: Pass
* Essay topic appears focused—not too general or too narrow.
* There are three clear main ideas.
* All three main ideas appear to support the topic.
* Each paragraph contains two to three details.
* All details appear related to the topic.
* Outline is presented neatly with very few writing errors.

Score 1: Needs More Work
* Essay topic is not completely clear—too general or too narrow.
* The three main ideas are incomplete.
* The three main ideas may not appear to support the topic.
* Each paragraph may contain fewer than three details.
* Details may appear unrelated to their main idea or overlap.
* Outline may not be presented neatly and/or may contain writing errors.

Score 0: No Response

Who's Your Audience?

Now that you have a structure for your essay, you're almost ready to look at the writing elements of an essay. However, you still have one important step: you must decide who your audience is. *To whom are you writing this piece?* In most cases, you're writing to your teacher, but it doesn't have to be that way! What if you write an essay describing how polluted your local beach is? What if you want to impress upon your community that everyone should do a better job picking up litter and avoiding toxic chemicals? If so, then your audience extends beyond your teacher. In fact, you might consider sending this kind of essay (which is persuasive) to your local newspaper. They might publish it!

This matter is important because both topic and audience should largely determine the tone of your essay. If you write about beach pollution, you will probably have a more assertive tone than if you write on different kinds of trees in your area. Likewise, your audience tells you what level of writing you should use. If you were writing a beach pollution paper for a group of fellow students, you would use different kinds of words than you would if writing to a group of adults or a class of third grade students, wouldn't you?

Look at the following two paragraphs. Can you identify the nature of the intended audience? Which one is intended for you?

> *Walking along the beautiful shoreline, I was taken in by the beauty of the crashing waves. Then suddenly, I felt a strong pinch under my foot. To my horror, I had stepped on a piece of glass from a soda bottle. I limped over to the lifeguard's tower, and as I did I noticed how much trash was littering the beach. Can't we do something about this?*

> *According to environmental impact reports, the volume of trash along our local shorelines has increased twofold in the last three years. This is an especially deleterious fact, given the assumed increase in environmental consciousness in our community. If we are to remedy the situation, we must take concrete steps, including appropriate legislation.*

Audience Exercises

1. Find copies of at least three different magazines. Here is a partial list to consider: (a) *Highlights* (b) *The Wall Street Journal* (c) *Scholastic* (d) *People* (e) *Time* (f) *Sports Illustrated*. Read one article from these and explain what kind of audience the article is intended for.

   Note: It is also interesting to study the advertising in each magazine. It will tell you much about the intended audience.

2. On the following page, you will write three paragraphs about the same topic. (This can be any topic you choose, including your essay topic.) However, you will write them to three different audiences. Include the same information in all three. This exercise shows how important it is to identify your intended audience, and how much it can change the way you write.

Who's Your Audience? *(cont.)*

Topic: _____

To Members of Your City Council:

_____

_____

_____

_____

_____

To Your Class:

_____

_____

_____

_____

_____

To Third Grade Students:

_____

_____

_____

_____

_____

Writing Paragraphs

Paragraphs are the building blocks of your essay. This is especially true in a format as straightforward as the five-paragraph essay. Each paragraph counts as its own unit and serves a unique purpose. In your outline, you have already structured your paragraphs by providing a main topic followed by three details. But that's only part of the equation—now you have to write these ideas down in a smooth manner.

The Structure of the Paragraph

In your outline, you have already established how your paragraphs are going to be structured by ordering the details. The first sentence of each paragraph is called the *topic sentence*. It can be seen as a mini-introduction to the paragraph itself. It simply states the main topic. This is followed by *supporting sentences* which develop or support the topic sentence. These ideas can be one or more sentences—whatever you need to get the point across. This is followed up by a *concluding sentence* which brings closure to the paragraph. In a sense, the paragraph itself is structured like a mini-essay, isn't it?

Returning to our outline on health food for kids, let's practice writing an effective paragraph, beginning with the first paragraph of the body of our essay. Here is what our outline looks like:

> **Main Idea:** Breakfast
>
> **Detail:** granola
>
> **Detail:** "Rice Dream" instead of milk!
>
> **Detail:** oatmeal

Now our job is to put these ideas into sentences:

> *[Topic] There are lots of healthful alternatives to the standard sugary or cholesterol-filled breakfast. [Supporting] To begin with, when most of us think of granola, our taste buds go dry. However, you'll be surprised at the variety and flavors of granola. Strawberry, cinnamon, and caramel are only a few that you can find. Not only are they good for you, but they also taste great. [Supporting] Suppose you have that delicious granola. Now, you're going to put some milk into it, right? Not so fast! Too much milk can be bad for you. What about trying "Rice Dream?" It's made from rice, and it's sweeter than milk. It goes great with cereal. [Supporting] Finally, for those of us who like hot breakfasts, oatmeal with a touch of maple syrup or honey is the only way to go. [Concluding] So, with that healthful menu for breakfast, you're ready to start your day.*

Notice how the details in the outline were made into sentence form, and in some cases embellished to further the point. As you can see, you are encouraged to make your essay colorful and detailed.

Using Transitions

In our sample paragraph about eating a healthful breakfast, notice how the series of ideas flow together. They do so with the help of *transitions*. There are four that do the work: *to begin with, not only, finally, and so*. Can you find them? Can you see how such transitions help link the ideas so that they relate to one another?

Now try reading the paragraphs without the transitions. It sounds strange, doesn't it? Without effective transitions, your paragraphs will come across as disconnected, as a series of facts without any relationship. Transitions link ideas so that they relate to one another; they provide comparison and contrast, and they strengthen and weaken ideas.

Keep in mind that you need transitions between paragraphs, too. Notice the transitions used in the sample essays on pages 39 and 41.

In some cases, transitions are single words. Other times they consist of more than one word, in which case they are called *transitional phrases*.

Study the list of transitions below.

above	finally	moreover
according to	first, second . . .	nevertheless
after	for example	next
also	for instance	obviously
although	furthermore	of course
another	however	similarly
because	in addition to	since
beside(s)	in fact	therefore
clearly	last	while
consequently	meanwhile	yet

As you can see, transitions serve all sorts of purposes. Once you get accustomed to using them, they will become second nature, and you will achieve a more fluid writing style.

Note: When transitions begin a sentence, they often require the use of a comma.

> *There is a lot left to be done.* **For example,** *we have to clean the house.*

Note: Transitions and transitional phrases don't always have to appear at the beginning of a sentence.

> *It is,* **however,** *important to vote when you turn eighteen.*

Using Transitions *(cont.)*

Transitions Exercise

Add appropriate transitions to the following essay. You can draw from the list on page 24, or you may use others.

Use Your Head

It is extremely important for motorcyclists to wear helmets. _____ if you crash on your motorcycle, chances are that a helmet could help save your life, so it makes sense to wear one. _____ taxpayers often have to help pay the cost of treating riders with serious head injuries, injuries that could have been avoided with the use of a helmet. _____ innocent passengers, oftentimes children, are injured. Wearing a helmet, _____ , makes absolute sense if you are riding a motorcycle.

_____ , helmets should be used while riding a bicycle. Statistics show, _____ , that bike riders are ten times more likely to suffer serious injury if they don't wear a helmet. _____ , helmet laws in our town require that only kids must wear helmets while riding a bike. This makes no sense. _____ , adults should model sensible behavior and wear helmets, too.

_____ , helmets should be worn by skateboarders. There are three reasons for this: _____ , skaters often practice their tricks on the street or in parking lots, where they can get hit by a car. _____ , while skaters don't ride as fast as bikers or motorcycle riders, they can have pretty bad wipe-outs. Just last week a friend of mine went into the hospital with a concussion from a skating accident. _____ , older skaters are role models for all the ten-year-olds out there. My little sister is already trying 360s. Because I wear a helmet, so does she.

_____ , helmets make sense. Whether you're riding the freeway on your motorcycle, peddling off on your bicycle, or spinning on your skateboard, you should use your head and wear a helmet!

Introductions and Conclusions

In a five-paragraph essay, the introduction and conclusion are very important. After all, they represent 40 percent of your essay!

Introductions

The *introduction* of a paper serves two purposes: (1) It clarifies what the essay is about, and (2) it grabs the reader's interest. The first goal is straightforward. The second one is more challenging.

Think about a few of your favorite movies. Now think about how they begin. You'll probably discover that most movies begin with a dramatic or suspenseful opening. This is called a *hook*. Whether it's a bit of slapstick humor or a violent encounter, the hook is intended to get you involved with the story right away and keep you watching. This same principle applies to essay writing.

Now, this does not mean that you have to have a sensational opening, but it should interest the reader by *showing—not telling*. Let's look at two versions of introductions to open our "Health Food for Kids" paper. Which one does a better job of introducing the essay? Which one would make you want to continue reading?

> *Kids eat a lot of food that is really bad for them. They eat so much junk food that they get used to it and think it's the way they're supposed to eat. They eat candy and chew gum, too. In this essay I am going to write about different healthful foods that are also tasty. After all, "you are what you eat."*

> *The sugar-coated purple cereal is disappearing as you slurp it down with chocolate milk. You jam some bubble gum in your mouth and hop on your bike. After hanging out at your friend's house, you get hungry and head for the nearest fast-food joint for your hamburger, fries, and Coke. Does this sound familiar? There are too many kids who eat very unhealthful foods and do not know there are tasty foods that are not bad for them. So, do yourself a favor and read ahead for a healthful menu for breakfast, lunch, and dinner.*

The first paragraph does a good job of clarifying the topic and explaining how the essay will progress. It's a fine introduction. The second version, however, is much more interesting, isn't it? It begins with a story line and grabs the reader's interest. The words are lively, and we are *shown* someone eating instead of being told about it.

Introductions and Conclusions *(cont.)*

Introductions *(cont.)*

The second introduction also gives you an idea of how the paper will proceed. Of course, you don't have to write something quite so dramatic. Here's another possibility:

> *What do you think of when you hear the words "health food?" Most kids think of food that tastes bad. After eating a health food candy bar, one of my friends said it tasted like cardboard. However, not all health food tastes bad. Here is a healthful menu for kids to choose from.*

This is another very good version. It is not a story line, but it uses good comparisons and begins with a question that gets the reader involved.

Conclusions

The primary purpose of your *conclusion* is to bring your paper to an end, to "wrap it up." Like introductions, good conclusions are interesting, leaving the reader with a strong sense of the paper. You should mention the points you just covered, but you don't need to "spell them out." This can be done a number of ways. Let's compare two conclusions for our health foods essay.

> *In conclusion, eating healthful foods makes a lot of sense. Those kids who continue to eat junk food all the time will only end up with bad eating habits when they get older. The foods for breakfast, lunch, and dinner that I have listed are great alternatives to unhealthful foods. You should always remember that "you are what you eat!"*

> *So, the next time you pop that jaw breaker into your mouth, the next time you eat oily potato chips for dinner, remember that there are tasty choices that **won't hurt your body**. Melons taste a lot like candy if you haven't been eating white sugar from those little packets every time you go to a restaurant. It might take a little getting used to, but once you begin to eat a healthful breakfast, lunch, and dinner, you'll feel and look better.*

The first conclusion is okay. It uses the helpful phrase "In conclusion" and reminds the reader what he or she just read. But notice how the second example is livelier. It also brings the essay to a close while keeping the reader involved. It also has the same kind of story line as the second introduction. This is called an *envelope strategy*, which is common in essay and story writing. You open and close your essay in the same way. This helps give your essay a sense of order.

Final Tip: As long as you have a good outline, it's often best to leave the writing of the introduction and conclusion until *after* you have written the body (three main idea paragraphs) of the paper. Once you see the details down on paper, it's easier to write engaging openings and closings.

Introductions and Conclusions *(cont.)*

Introductions and Conclusions Exercises

1. Below you will find an introduction and a conclusion for an essay on computers. Rewrite them, bringing them to life by showing instead of telling. Consider using the envelope strategy. Share your versions with your classmates.

Introduction

Computers are changing the way we live. Computers have become very important in day-to-day life. This is especially true in the workplace, where computers are a necessity. In this essay, I will show you some of the major ways computers have changed the way we live.

Conclusion

In conclusion, I have shown how computers have caused great changes to come about in society. Both our home life and our work life have been changed by e-mail, the Internet, and so forth. In the future, there will probably be even more changes.

2. For each of the following topics, write an attractive introduction and conclusion.

A. Racism

_____

_____

_____

_____

B. Chocolate

_____

_____

_____

_____

C. Vacations

_____

_____

_____

_____

Writing Your Rough Draft

Now that you have settled on a structure and learned to write engaging introductions and conclusions, it's time to begin your rough draft. A *rough draft* represents your *first attempt to write* your paper. In this draft, it's important to remember that while you are trying to write well, your main focus is to get the essay written, to get your ideas down clearly.

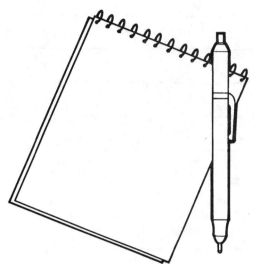

We will take this process slowly, focusing on one paragraph at a time. Following the details on your outline, we will first focus on the three main idea paragraphs, the body of your paper. When you finish your rough draft, review what you learned on pages 26 and 27, and then write an engaging opening and closing to your paper. As we mentioned earlier, it is easier to write these sections last.

On the following pages, there are a series of questions beneath each paragraph. Once you are finished with each paragraph, answer this list of questions. They will help ensure that you have your main ideas down and that your paragraph reflects your outline.

The best thing about writing a rough draft is that when you are finished, you have your essay before you. Even if it's not up to par yet, you have something to work with! If you are not used to writing more than one draft, however, this might take some adjustment. There is a tendency (and temptation) to think it's done the first time around.

There are a few things to consider when writing your first draft:

- **Don't worry about getting it perfect.** A rough draft represents your first try, so don't get bogged down by the nitty-gritty yet. That will be handled during the revision process. If you write a sentence that doesn't come out right, if you can't quite explain what you mean, don't spend too much time wrestling with it here. As long as the idea is written down, you will return to these issues once the draft is complete. You will find that it's much easier to rework parts of your essay once the whole first draft is done. So, as you are writing your rough draft, always remember that you can change it!

- **Get all your ideas on paper. Follow your outline.** You worked hard on your outline. Now, be sure your hard work pays off by including, in order, all your supporting points. Likewise, you should "go for it" in your rough draft. Express your ideas fully. Once again you can always whittle away at it later.

- **Rough does not mean sloppy!** Although this is your first draft, it is an attempt to write your paper well and with care.

Writing Your Rough Draft *(cont.)*

Rough Draft: Main Idea Paragraph #1

_____

_____

_____

_____

_____

_____

_____

_____

_____

_____

_____

_____

_____

_____

_____

_____

_____

_____

Answer the following questions:
- Do I have a clear topic sentence?
- Do all my ideas and details from my outline appear here?
- Is there a clear distinction between my details?
- Do I use transitions to link ideas?
- Do I have a clear concluding sentence?

Writing Your Rough Draft *(cont.)*

Rough Draft: Main Idea Paragraph #2

_____

_____

_____

_____

_____

_____

_____

_____

_____

_____

_____

_____

_____

_____

_____

_____

_____

_____

_____

_____

Answer the following questions:
- Do I have a clear topic sentence?
- Do all my ideas and details from my outline appear here?
- Is there a clear distinction between my details?
- Do I use transitions to link ideas?
- Do I have a clear concluding sentence?

Writing Your Rough Draft *(cont.)*

Rough Draft: Main Idea Paragraph #3

_____

_____

_____

_____

_____

_____

_____

_____

_____

_____

_____

_____

_____

_____

_____

_____

_____

Answer the following questions:
- Do I have a clear topic sentence?
- Do all my ideas and details from my outline appear here?
- Is there a clear distinction between my details?
- Do I use transitions to link ideas?
- Do I have a clear concluding sentence?

Editing, Revising, and Rewriting

Now that you have your first draft complete, you are ready to move on to some of the "nitty-gritty" work of writing: revising. *Revision* means to "look again." This is exactly what we will be doing. You are going to study your paper, making sure that all the elements we have covered are executed well. Why? Because, as any experienced writer will tell you, *rewriting is the key to writing well!* Many beginning writers think that when they're done with the first draft, their work is over. However, the first draft is only the beginning. Now it's time to sharpen your writing, to make sure your ideas are clear and balanced.

An important element of revising your paper is called *editing*. When you edit, you mark the mistakes on your draft. These might range from spelling and punctuation errors to awkward sounding sentences. The key to successful editing is to slow down, take the essay line by line and proofread very carefully.

You should also whittle away at material that is overwritten or that appears unnecessary. However, if you think some ideas need more information and embellishment, this is the time to add it.

When you finish revising, you move to *rewriting* the essay. Here, you take out your pen (or computer) and, using your revising and editing notes, you rewrite your paper. In some cases your rewrite will look very different from your original rough draft.

Let's begin by outlining our approach to revision, which is going to be a three-part process. Follow these instructions carefully.

1. Using the guidelines listed on the following pages, edit, revise, and rewrite the sample essay "Desert Life" on page 36. Give the rewrite to your teacher.

2. Applying the strategies that you have learned, revise and rewrite your essay.

3. Once your draft is done, your teacher will help you with the peer editing process. You will give your essay to three classmates for their peer editing responses. You will, in turn, receive three essays to read.

For each essay you read, fill in the Peer Response Sheet. When you peer edit, read your classmates' essays carefully. The goal here is to provide constructive feedback. Peer editing also gives you the opportunity to see other writing approaches and styles. When you write responses to your peers' works, you should strive to be honest yet constructive. Remember, *you are trying to help the writers make their papers better.*

Once you receive the three peer editing responses to your essay, you will write your final draft. Study the peer responses carefully. Consider all your classmates' suggestions. If any of them ring true, or if all three readers commented on the same thing, go ahead and make changes in your paper.

Note: On page 35, you will find a list of standard editing notations. Using them can make your task easier and faster.

Editing, Revising, and Rewriting (cont.)

Editing and Revision Response Sheet Questions

Study the following sets of questions carefully. When you begin your revision process, use the questions as a checklist. As you can see, the first questions deal primarily with the ideas in the paper. The second set involves punctuation, spelling, and grammar. Be sure to have a piece of paper with you to take notes.

1. Does the essay have an attractive title? Does the title give the reader a clear idea of what to expect?

2. Is the introduction engaging? Does it give the reader a clear idea of how the essay will unfold?

3. Is the conclusion engaging? Does it remind the reader what he or she has just read, bringing the essay to a smooth close?

4. Does the essay flow? Are transitions used effectively?

5. Is the structure logical? Are the ideas related?

6. Is there a balance of emphasis in all three paragraphs? Does one paragraph seem to get a lot more attention than the others?

7. Are there parts that need more (or less) explanation?

8. Is the tone of the essay appropriate? Is it spirited? Does it involve the reader?

9. Is the writing clear? Does it make sense to you?

10. Do the ideas ever go off in too many directions? Are there any tangents or "side roads" along the way?

11. Are the details lively and appropriate?

12. Is there anything in the essay that is unclear? Is there anything that needs more definition or explaining?

13. Are all words spelled correctly? Proofread!

14. Is the grammar correct? Are there any run-on sentences that need to be rewritten?

15. Are the sentences clear? Are there any awkward sentences that need to be rewritten?

16. Are there opportunities to use more precise words? Are there words that are repeated too much?

17. Are there cliches? Cliches are phrases like "last, but not least," or "raining cats and dogs."

Editing, Revising, and Rewriting *(cont.)*

Editor's Marks

Here is a list of editor's marks to use while you proofread. Although they take a little while to learn, they will save you time in the long run. They serve as a common code that writers and editors use to indicate errors wherever English is written.

Remember that when you edit, you are looking at all areas of writing mechanics. These include capitalization, punctuation, sentence run-ons and fragments, commas, quotation marks, new paragraph indentations (or spacing), and spelling.

Editor's Mark	Meaning	Example
℮	Delete	It was ~~was~~ very tiny.
≡	Capitalize	the boy ran quickly.
/	Use lowercase	Many Athletes ran in the marathon.
∧	Add a word	I want an ice ∧cream sundae.
RO	Run-on sentence	Who's there RO what do you want?
frag.	Sentence fragment	Although the peddler's cart. frag.
SP	Spelling error	Monkies SP swung in the trees.
∽	Reverse letters or words	Five books on were the shlef.
⊙	Add a period	Children played all day⊙
∧,	Add a comma	I like apples∧peaches and pears.
∨'	Add an apostrophe	John's puppy is cute.
ⱽ⁝ ⱽ⁝	Add quotation marks	Help! I cried.
¶	Begin a new paragraph	"Hello," said Carla.¶ "Hi," Beth replied.
#	Make a space	I love French#fries.
◡	Close the space	He lives in the country side.
stet	Do not delete (Let it stand.)	The ~~beautiful~~ swan flew away.

Editing, Revising, and Rewriting *(cont.)*

Directions: Use the editor's marks from page 35 to edit the following essay.

Desert Life

The desert is really full of life. Which is not what most people think because when they think of the dessert all they think of is sand and snakes and stuff like that. In this essay I am going to explain how the desert really is full of life and not a wasteland.

First, there are lots and lots of different types of animals it the desert for example, there are desert tortoises. If you see one make sure you leave it alone because they might be going extinct. There are also a variety of desert birds, not only ravens and crows but also hawks. Lizards and snakes and horned toads are common inhabitants, too.

Second, the desert has very different and dramatic seasons. Not only hot. There is the winter, where in high deserts you can get snow and it can get below freezing. In springtime there are wildflowers.

Third, there are lots of people who live in the desert and lots of history there too. People have always lived in the desert, in fact lots of the middle east is desert. Nowadays, with more and more people being born, there are cities springing up in the desert like oases! The pioneers came across deserts in their covered wagons and left behind many artifacts that can still be seen in places and native americans have lived in the desert for centuries. The Pioneers were very brave, and had to endure many hardships. Can you imagine crossing snow-covered mountains in a wagon?

In conclusion, the desert is really full of life. There are animals, seasons, and people inhabiting it. As you can see, it's not really a wasteland at all. Maybe you can convince your parents to take you there for vacation, but probably not in the summer!

Editing, Revising, and Rewriting *(cont.)*

Peer Response Sheet

Your Name:_____

Author's Name: _____

Place an X under the appropriate place on the provided lines.

                                               Very Much   Somewhat

1. I enjoyed reading this. _____

2. This made sense to me. _____

3. The writing is clear. _____

Finish the following statements as best you can. Remember, your job is to help the writer.

1. One thing I really like about the writing is . . . _____

_____

_____

_____

2. One thing I think the author can improve on is . . . _____

_____

_____

_____

3. Something I would like the author to tell more about is . . . _____

_____

_____

_____

4. My other comment is . . . _____

_____

_____

_____

Final Draft Rubric

(See page 20 for an explanation of how to use a rubric.)

Score 3: High Pass
- Student presents essay neatly.
- Student follows his or her outline clearly.
- Student's writing is very clear and free of spelling, grammar, and punctuation errors.
- Student makes excellent use of transitions.
- Introduction and conclusion are engaging.
- Paragraphs are clearly structured units.
- Details are rich and specific.
- Student's writing is spirited.
- Student's essay is more than a presentation of facts. Some guiding interest, or "angle," is achieved.
- Student demonstrates mastery of the five-paragraph form.

Score 2: Pass
- Student presents essay neatly.
- Student follows his or her outline clearly.
- Student's writing is clear and almost completely free of spelling, grammar, and punctuation errors.
- Student makes effective use of transitions.
- Introduction and conclusion are clear and inviting.
- Paragraphs are clearly structured units.
- Details are specific and do not overlap.
- Student's writing may be spirited.
- Student's essay may be more than a presentation of facts.
- Student demonstrates good understanding of the five-paragraph form.

Score 1: Needs More Work
- Student may present essay neatly.
- Student may not follow his or her outline clearly.
- Student's writing may not be clear and may contain spelling, grammar, and punctuation errors.
- Student may not make effective use of transitions.
- Introduction and conclusion may be too brief and/or unclear.
- Paragraphs may not be clearly structured units.
- Details may be too general and may overlap.
- Student's writing may not be spirited and may appear rushed.
- Student's essay may appear solely as a presentation of facts.
- Student may not demonstrate a good understanding of the five-paragraph form.

Score 0: No Response

Sample Essays

Emily's First Year

Last night my mother came back from the hospital with Emily, my new baby sister. As I looked at Emily's tiny feet and her dark hair, I wondered how soon she will recognize me. When will she start talking? When will she take her first step? When will she start eating food? So, I decided to find out. To my amazement, she will change more than I could imagine. Here are just a few of the changes in behavior I can expect in the first twelve months of Emily's life.

In Emily's first four months, she will change so much. Early on, she will not be able to focus more than a few feet away. She will not be able to hold a rattle. She will want to be cuddled and loved and spoken to. By the second month she will be able to see Mom, and by the fourth month she will probably be able to follow Fido (our dog) around with her eyes. After four months, she will be shaking that rattle and maybe even gathering up toys. She will start playing with her hands and making different sounds for different needs. She will even start laughing.

In the next four months of her first year, Emily will learn to sit up by herself, and she will probably enjoy sitting in a high chair. She will learn to crawl across the carpet in our living room, and by pulling herself up on our couch, learn to stand on her two feet. She will probably start eyeing that carrot or cracker and try feeding herself (messy!). She will also start playing by herself, trying to figure things out, like how to pick up a third block when two are already in her hand. I can't wait until she plays peekaboo! Even though she will be more independent, she will still want to be held. To let us know this, she will lift up those pudgy little arms.

In the final part of Emily's first year, she will start "power crawling" across the house. We'll have to keep an eye on her because she'll be poking at things and trying to pull on chords and turn the volume knob on the stereo. I'm sure Dad will love it if she starts saying "da-da," which is very likely. She will understand what "no" means, and she will remember where the refrigerator is and who we're talking about when we say "Mama's coming." When I take her to the sandbox to play, she will enjoy filling and dumping sand, as long as I can keep her from throwing it in my eyes. Finally, I shouldn't be surprised if, any day now, she gets up and walks!

Mom, Dad, and I have the video camera ready to go. I've decided to start a journal to follow Emily's first year. The journal will be her birthday present when she turns one. I can't believe this tiny baby swaddled in a blanket will be waving bye-bye and, just maybe, walking along on her own within one short year.

Sample Essays *(cont.)*

Reading Response to "Emily's First Year"

Structure: How is this essay structured? How does the writer use Emily's growth process to help point the way to an outline? How does each of the paragraphs unfold? Are there similarities between them?

_____

_____

_____

Writing: Is the writing clear? Are there parts that are hard to follow? Does the writer ever repeat herself? Are there passages that you really like?

_____

_____

_____

Details: What kinds of details does the writer use to get her point across? How does she make them interesting? Does the writer explain where she got her information?

_____

_____

_____

Audience: Who is the intended audience for this essay?

_____

General Impressions: Did you enjoy reading this essay? What did you like in particular? Are there areas that can be improved? Do you have any suggestions?

_____

_____

_____

_____

Sample Essays *(cont.)*

The Art of Waking Up

The beeping of your alarm clock always starts too early. You hit the "sleep" button and bury your head under your pillow, but it's no use. In a minute your dad is knocking on your door. "Time for school," he says. As you lift your sleepy body from under the covers, you have only one thought: "There must be an easier way." As a fellow student who must wake up far earlier than he wants, I have thought of the following steps to making getting up from bed and getting ready for school a less painful experience.

The most important step is shaking off that drowsiness that lingers in your bones. There are several good approaches. You can use the cold-water-on-the-face strategy, which always works but also causes shuddering and can be shocking. If your parents allow it, you can try jumping on your bed. For those who must, there's always the long and leisurely shower. However, this requires the sacrifice of an extra few minutes of sleep time. Do not spend too much time in a warm shower, as it may have an opposite effect and make you <u>more</u> tired.

Now that you are at least partially conscious, it's time to take that next important step: to eat breakfast. While everyone has his or her own tastes in food, I do have some recommendations, as well as some eating tips. First of all, avoid the rushed breakfast. Jamming a piece of toast in your mouth while you run off to catch the bus is not fun. Secondly, make sure that your kitchen is stocked with breakfast foods you like. There is nothing more disappointing than craving oatmeal with maple syrup only to find yourself eating corn flakes. Finally, make sure to eat a hearty breakfast that gives you the energy you will need for the day. A tall glass of orange juice is highly recommended. This leads us to our final waking-up skill: preparation.

If you have ever wakened to discover that you can't find your notebook, you don't have a shirt to wear, your hair's a mess, or your bike has a flat, you know what I am talking about here. After all, how can you wake up in style if you're busy rushing around looking for a folder or catching up on math problems? For that reason, it is important that you complete all of your homework the night before and then place all your schoolbooks neatly in your backpack. Leave the backpack beside the door so you can grab it in the morning. It is also good to choose your wardrobe and lay it out neatly where it can be seen when you wake up. Your other duty is to tie up loose ends and be ready for anything. Did you feed the dog? What if it's raining? Do you know where your umbrella is?

Now that you have this valuable information, your school day wake-ups will be more pleasant instead of a sudden thump on the head. Rather than hurrying and getting ready for school, you will wake up with a strategy to shake off your drowsiness, eat a healthful breakfast, and get to school without delays. Just make sure it's not Saturday!

Sample Essays *(cont.)*

Reading Response to "The Art of Waking Up"

Structure: How is this essay structured? How does each of the paragraphs unfold? Are there similarities between them?

_____

_____

_____

Writing: Is the writing clear? Are there parts that are hard to follow? Does the writer ever repeat herself? Are there passages that you really like?

_____

_____

_____

Details: What kinds of details does the writer use to get her point across? How does she make them interesting? Does the writer explain where she got her information?

_____

_____

_____

Audience: Who is the intended audience for this essay?

_____

General Impressions: Did you enjoy reading this essay? What did you like in particular? Are there areas that can be improved? Do you have any suggestions?

_____

_____

_____

_____

Presenting Your Essay

You have worked hard on writing your essay. You have gathered ideas and shaped them into a well-structured and well-written paper. Now, instead of burying your composition in your notebook, you have the opportunity to present it to your classmates. In short, you will give a speech! This is a great way to practice your speaking skills and to learn more about your classmates' topics. Before starting, look at a few presentation tips below.

Presentation Tips

- **Practice reading your essay aloud:** Most of us get a little nervous when we stand in front of a group of people. That's why you should practice reading your essay until it's very familiar to you. Then, when your heart starts to flutter, you can anchor yourself to the words that are fresh in your mind.

- **Make eye contact:** Eye contact helps you establish a relationship with your audience. Our tendency, especially if we're nervous, is to always stare at our paper. Making eye contact is not always comfortable, but it's an important part of delivering an effective presentation. Finally, be sure to vary your point of focus. We tend to lock eyes onto one person (often, the teacher!) or one group.

- **Speak slowly and loudly:** When we're nervous, we tend to rush through our words or to mumble softly. That's why it's important to focus on enunciating and projecting your voice outward. This will ensure that your audience hears you and understands you. Remember that you need to reach the person sitting farthest away from you.

- **Use visual aids:** Whether it's an overhead projection showing a graph or an object that involves your topic, a visual aid is always a welcome addition to a presentation. For the "Health Food for Kids" topic, for example, the student might conclude his or her presentation by serving some delectable health foods. One warning: Don't allow your visual aid to take attention away from your essay. Use the visual aid at the appropriate time.

- **Bring in a guest speaker:** In this case, ask your teacher if it's okay to bring in an expert on your topic. After you present your essay, invite questions for the guest.

Publishing an Essay Anthology

A fun "wrap-it-up" project involves making a class essay anthology. An *anthology* is a collection of literary works. This will take a lot of teamwork and will give you a taste of what book publishers go through. When the books are done, each of you will have an essay anthology to remember your class by.

Let's look at the eight different "departments" needed to put our book together. These groups should meet to discuss the project *before* putting the book together, and then report back to the group. In some cases, decisions will conflict and should be left to the discretion of the teacher.

Be sure to meet as a whole class regularly so that the lines of communication are clear. Good luck!

Budget

You will be surprised to find how much it can cost to put together 20 or 30 anthologies. Whether or not you will use color and what kind of binding you will have all depends on the cost of copies.

Before you begin your project, establish your budget with your teacher. It's the job of the budgeting department to collect receipts and discuss the cost of the various steps. For example, it might cost an extra $30.00 to have color on the cover. Do you have the money for this?

The budget department should also look for money-saving opportunities. Is there a class parent who runs a printing shop? Can you sell some of the anthologies?

Collectors

This group of people is responsible for gathering everyone's essays by a certain deadline. If one of the contributors is lax, then it's a collector's responsibility to call him or her on the phone and get a clean copy of the essay to the group!

Writers

Although most of the book is already written, there is more to be done. Someone needs to put together a table of contents, a title page, a copyright page, and, if desired, a dedication. Depending on the decisions of the cover design group, some writing might appear on the back cover. It's the responsibility of this group to attend to these matters.

Editors

These people are the "bosses" of the project. They must make a number of very important decisions: How will the essays be ordered? Alphabetically? By topic? Will there be illustrations or graphics in the book? If so, should they all be original student art? Will the essays appear back to back? What will the book be titled? How many copies should be made? (Check with budgeting!)

Publishing an Essay Anthology *(cont.)*

Editors *(cont.)*

When departments have trouble making a decision, the editors have the last word. They also have the responsibility to look through every essay, making sure there are no major errors, like missing paragraphs. They are *not* responsible for proofreading—that's each author's job.

If it helps, you might want to break the editors into different groups: type, illustrations, and so forth.

Layout

In publishing terms, *layout* means "the process of arranging printed or graphic matter on a page." This involves all sorts of decisions: What size of page do you want? Should all the fonts and sizes be the same? Where should the page numbers appear? If graphics or illustrations are going to be used, where should they appear? Should they be enlarged? Reduced?

As you can see, layout is a lot of work.

Naturally, these decisions should be made *before* you hand in the essays for publishing.

Cover Design

The front and back covers of the book are very important. They give the reader a first impression. This doesn't mean that they have to be fancy, but the cover design group should decide on how to make the cover appealing. This depends partly on your resources. Here are some important questions for the cover design people:

Do you want an illustration on the cover? What about some writing on the back cover? Have you studied other anthologies to get ideas?

Publishing and Binding

While the rest of the class is busy putting the book together, this group is researching how best to publish the book. The book can be bound a number of ways, from using a three-hole punch and inserting brads, to having them "perfect bound." Again, it's going to depend on your time and resources. So, once the "master copy" of the class anthology is ready to go, it is handed over to this group.

Distribution

This group is responsible for getting the anthology distributed. If you have made copies for other teachers or classrooms, this group delivers them. Perhaps you will want to send one to your local newspaper.

Other Types of Essays

The five-paragraph form is a very useful introduction to essay writing. It is the first step in learning to write a clear, organized essay. However, it is only the first step in the essay writing process. As you move along in school, you will learn about a number of different kinds of essays. Also, your pieces will get longer and more involved. Here is a sampling of three more types of essays and some of their features. You can practice all three in the five-paragraph framework.

Argument Essay

Most essays are persuasive in nature—that is, the writer is trying to convince the reader of something, even if it's factual. If I am writing about the fact that dinosaurs had a variety of eating habits, I am still trying to *convince* the reader that it is true.

The argument essay takes this step further by taking a side on an issue. Let's say I believe that the Internet should be censored, or that jazz is better than country music. Either belief would make a perfect topic for an argument essay.

In an argument essay, the skills we have just learned are important. The writer must have lots of good details to support his or her side. Furthermore, the writer must consider the side of the opposition and explain why it's wrong! Most newspapers and magazines feature these essays, some in the form of *editorials*, which are articles that express an opinion about a current issue.

Compare and Contrast Essay

When you write a compare and contrast essay, you highlight the similarities (comparison) and differences (contrast) between two subjects. Suppose you just moved from elementary to middle school. The similarities and differences between the two would make a perfect topic. What if you collect Beanie Babies and Barbies? Comparing and contrasting them would be interesting, wouldn't it?

While comparing and contrasting can be strictly for information, it can also be used to answer a question. For example, which is a better place for an aspiring actor to live: Los Angeles or New York? Should you collect stamps or coins? The purpose of the compare and contrast paper would be to highlight the features of each in order to answer the question.

Personal Experience Essay

This essay relies on personal experiences rather than information from outside sources. Your job here is to highlight an event that was important in your life, describing it in a meaningful way. For example, let's say you're writing about a camping trip. It involved hiking 50 miles with a heavy backpack. You were miserable much of the time, but to your surprise you finished and afterwards felt very satisfied. The essay would describe the events in an organized way, explaining why it was meaningful to you and how it helped you push yourself beyond your limits.

Writing a Collective Essay

Now that you have put so much work into your essay, it is time to have some fun with essay writing. All you need is five students, a piece of paper, a pencil or pen, and your imagination. The objective here is to write an essay together, with each person taking one paragraph of the five. However, there is a catch: when it's your turn to write, *all you will be able to read is the final line of the previous paragraph!*

The process goes like this:

1. One person begins by writing a title and an introduction to the essay. (Decide among yourselves whether or not you want to establish the topic before you begin or leave it to the first writer.) He or she then folds the paper over, leaving *only the last line* of writing visible. This is passed on to the next person.

2. This person reads the last line and then proceeds to write the first main idea paragraph (that is, the second paragraph of the essay). Obviously, the new writer will have only a hint of what the topic is about!

3. Now, the process should continue until all five paragraphs are complete.

4. When you are finished, read the essay aloud. There will be lots of laughs, not to speak of surprises, because of "interesting" connections between ideas.

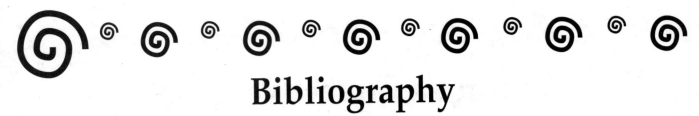

Bibliography

Applebee, Arthur. *Writing in the Secondary School.* National Council of Teachers of English, 1981.

Atwell, Nancie. *In the Middle: Writing, Reading, and Learning with Adolescents.* Boyton/Cook, 1987.

Caplan, Rebekah. *Writing in Training: A Guide to Developing a Composition Program for Language Arts Teachers.* Dale Seymour Publications, 1984.

Caulkins, Lucy. *The Art of Teaching Writing.* Heinemann, 1986.

Elbow, Peter. *Writing with Power: Techniques for Mastering the Writing Process.* Oxford University Press, 1981.

Graves, Donald. *Children Want to Write.* Heinemann, 1982.

Graves, Donald and Virginia Stuart. *Write from the Start.* Dutton, 1985.

Murray, Donald. *Writing to Learn.* Holt, Rinehart and Winston, 1984.

Muschla, Gary Robert. *Writing Workshop Survival Kit.* The Center for Applied Research in Education, 1993.

Silberman, Arlene. *Growing Up Writing: Teaching Children to Write, Think, and Learn.* Time Books, 1989.

Reading and Writing Links

A+ Research & Writing
http://www.ipl.org/teen/aplus/

MiddleZine
http://156.63.113.15/hms/acad/red/middlezine/index.html

The Vocal Point
http://bvsd.k12.co.us/schools/cent/Newspaper/Newspaper.html

The On-Line Books Page
http://www.cs.cmu.edu/books.html

The Complete Works of William Shakespeare
http://www-tech.mit.edu/Shakespeare/

The New York Times
http://www.nyt.com/

Diary Project
http://www.diaryproject.com/